The Teen Guide to Adulting: Gaining Financial Independence

What You Need to Know About

HEALTH INSURANCE

CAROL HAND

New York

Published in 2021 by The Rosen Publishing Group, Inc.
29 East 21st Street, New York, NY 10010

Copyright © 2021 by The Rosen Publishing Group, Inc.

First Edition

All rights reserved. No part of this book may be reproduced in any form without permission in writing from the publisher, except by a reviewer.

Library of Congress Cataloging-in-Publication Data

Names: Hand, Carol, 1945– author.
Title: What you need to know about health insurance / Carol Hand.
Description: First edition. | New York: Rosen Publishing, 2021. | Series: The teen guide to adulting: gaining financial independence | Audience: Grades 7 to 12. | Includes bibliographical references and index.
Identifiers: LCCN 2019011108| ISBN 9781725340572 (library bound) | ISBN 9781725340565 (pbk.)
Subjects: LCSH: Health insurance—Juvenile literature. | Health services accessibility—Economic aspects—United States—Juvenile literature. | Finance, Personal—Juvenile literature.
Classification: LCC HG9383 .H36 2021 | DDC 368.38/2—dc23
LC record available at https://lccn.loc.gov/2019011108

Manufactured in China

CONTENTS

INTRODUCTION................................4

CHAPTER ONE
WHO NEEDS HEALTH INSURANCE?...............7

CHAPTER TWO
TYPES OF HEALTH INSURANCE...................18

CHAPTER THREE
CHOOSING A HEALTH CARE PLAN................31

CHAPTER FOUR
SUPPLEMENTING HEALTH INSURANCE...........44

CHAPTER FIVE
COMPARING US HEALTH CARE...................55

GLOSSARY..66
FOR MORE INFORMATION.......................69
FOR FURTHER READING.........................72
BIBLIOGRAPHY...................................73
INDEX..77

INTRODUCTION

Holly Wood knows what it's like to live with health insurance and without it. When Wood was a teenager, her mother was a single parent working as a waitress and earning about $15,000 per year. The family was eligible for Medicaid, a government-sponsored health insurance program available only to low-income families. This eligibility was lucky for Wood. At age fourteen, she was diagnosed with an eating disorder and treated at a state facility. The bill totaled $60,000. At age fifteen, she had gall bladder surgery, which cost $17,000. In the week of high school graduation, her appendix burst, requiring surgery that totaled $20,000. During her teen years, her hospital bills added up to more than $100,000. Medicaid paid them all. Her mother could never have paid her medical expenses—they would have cost her entire salary for almost ten years.

But at age twenty, when Wood was in college, she was no longer eligible for Medicaid, and she could not afford health insurance. She went from being protected to feeling panic at every sore throat or stomachache. She did not participate in sports, for fear of being injured. She could not afford to see a dentist or buy birth control pills. Her friends who had health care took it for granted and could not understand her fear. By 2017, Wood was a graduate student at Harvard, and she had access to their excellent student health program. But she hasn't forgotten. Writing for Vox, Wood says, "Living in America

After passage of the Affordable Care Act (ACA) in 2010, many people became eligible for health care. But health care is expensive and many people still lack access.

without insurance brings with it the kind of fear that makes you avoid taking the bus because you fear catching a cold, which might turn into a respiratory infection, which could then become a stubborn pneumonia requiring an overnight hospital stay, which can cost the equivalent of several months' rent."

In 2013, according to the Kaiser Family Foundation, there were forty-four million uninsured nonelderly Americans in the United States. By 2016, the Affordable Care Act (ACA) had decreased this number to about twenty-seven million. In 2017, the number of uninsured increased again, by about 700,000 people, because of changes to the ACA or changes

INTRODUCTION

requiring work in exchange for Medicaid payments. It is often difficult for low- and middle-income Americans to find and keep affordable health insurance. Plus, the high cost of medical care means unexpected illness or injury can bankrupt a person. The number of bankruptcies each year because of medical costs is uncertain. In the ten years between 2007 and 2017, estimates ranged from a low of about 270,000 to a high of one million per year, depending on the year and the method of calculation.

Both health care and health insurance in the United States are expensive. Health insurance can be complicated to understand, and it changes every year. But it is vital for every adult, young and old. Starting early to understand health insurance and keeping updated on the changes will help tomorrow's young adults prepare for unexpected health challenges and avoid the fear caused by lack of insurance.

CHAPTER ONE

WHO NEEDS HEALTH INSURANCE?

Insurance is a form of financial protection against losses due to damage or injury. The person buying insurance is buying a contract, or agreement, with the insurance company. He or she pays an annual insurance premium to purchase a certain maximum payout. For example, an annual premium of $1,000 might pay for $50,000 of insurance. The company supplies an insurance policy stating the terms of the contract—such as the annual cost of the insurance, the specific items or activities that are protected, and the maximum payout to the insured if they suffer a loss. This process protects the insured person from unexpected situations. For example, if a car is totaled in an accident, the insured can file a claim and the insurance company will pay the value of the car. The person does not have to pay the whole cost of replacing the car.

An insurance company sells policies to many clients, but only a few clients will suffer a loss and file a claim (apply for a payout) each year. By spreading the risk among many clients, the insurance company takes in much more money in premiums than it pays out. This practice ensures that

Most US health insurance is sold by insurance companies, which must make a profit. Here, a person files a health insurance claim online.

the company makes a profit and stays in business. Auto, homeowners, life, and health are the most common types of insurance. Health insurance protects the insured against the costs of illness or injury.

THE LANGUAGE OF HEALTH INSURANCE

Health insurance has its own vocabulary; mastering some of this vocabulary makes it easier to navigate the field. The most basic aspects of health insurance are the insurance policy, a written description of the items and services covered; the insurance premium, or monthly cost of buying the insurance; and the insurance claim, a formal request from an insured person to the insurance company, requesting payment for an item or service. Benefits are the items and services paid for by the insurance. Low-income individuals and families may qualify for a subsidy, a government benefit that pays part of their premium.

Although health insurance often pays most of a person's medical costs, it seldom pays all. The amount left over—the amount for which the insured person is responsible—is referred to as out-of-pocket expenses. Types of out-of-pocket expenses include deductibles, co-payments, and coinsurance.

A deductible is the amount the insured must pay before the insurance company's help kicks in. If a policy has a deductible of $250, the patient pays the first $250 of medical expenses at the beginning of each year; then, the insurance company begins paying. These annual deductibles may be low (such as $250) or high (say, $2,000). If the deductible is higher, the premiums are lower. A co-payment is an amount the patient pays for every doctor visit or other service after paying the deductible. If a doctor visit costs $150, the patient might pay a $25 co-pay for every visit, and the insurance pays the rest. Coinsurance is similar, but is calculated as a percentage, rather than a fixed amount. For example, the patient might pay 20 percent of any bill—that is, $20 on a $100 medical bill, or $200 on a $1,000 bill.

Because medical care is extremely expensive, a serious illness or injury can easily bankrupt a person or family. The insurance industry has two basic methods to help protect people from serious debt. First, health insurance policies

Even if they have insurance, patients must pay deductibles, co-pay, and other parts of a hospital bill. Here, a hospital receptionist receives payment from a patient.

an out-of-pocket maximum, or limit. If a policy has a maximum of $4,000, the insured pays deductibles, coinsurance, and co-payments up to $4,000. Above that maximum, the insurance pays 100 percent of the covered expenses for the rest of the year. The insured must still pay for any medical costs not covered by the policy. Second, health care plans do not limit the yearly or lifetime amount insurance companies will spend on essential health benefits. After you reach the out-of-pocket maximum, the insurance company must pay 100 percent of your health care costs, no matter how high they are.

HEALTH INSURANCE? BUT I'M YOUNG AND HEALTHY!

Health insurance pays for medical and surgical expenses, including doctor visits, surgeries, and hospital stays. Often young, healthy people think they have no need for health insurance. But there are several good reasons to have it, even if it seems unnecessary.

First, bad things happen. A healthy young person might break a leg skiing, twist a knee playing football, or be involved in an auto accident. An unexpected flu or cold virus may lead to an emergency room visit. A person's appendix may burst, requiring surgery and a several-day hospital stay. Occasionally, even worse things happen: a previously healthy person may develop cancer, or meningitis, or another dangerous illness. Health insurance pays most of the expenses for these unexpected medical emergencies. Even young people who remain healthy have peace of mind, knowing that, if medical disaster does strike, their medical needs will be met.

Second, some people, although otherwise healthy, may have a chronic illness, such as diabetes, asthma, epilepsy, or depression. Medical treatment for such illnesses is necessary, ongoing, and often expensive. A person with a chronic illness should always have health insurance.

Third, health insurance pays for preventive care—care that keeps you healthy. This care includes services such as vaccinations, routine physical exams, and screenings for cancer, HIV, and other diseases. These services are sometimes entirely

A diabetic boy checks his blood sugar levels. People with chronic illnesses must always monitor their conditions and should have health insurance so medical treatment is always available.

covered by insurance; the patient pays nothing. Preventive care can help people catch health problems early, when their treatment is easier, less expensive, and more likely to result in a complete cure.

Fourth, young people without health insurance tend to put off seeing a doctor even when they need to. Suppose a person catches the flu, and it doesn't go away. She self-medicates with over-the-counter remedies, but remains ill. Eventually she collapses. She ends up in the hospital with pneumonia and a hefty hospital bill—all because she had no health insurance and didn't want to pay for a doctor visit. And, of course, without health insurance, she never got the flu shot that might have prevented her from getting sick.

Often, young people avoid getting health insurance because they fear the expense. There is always a monthly premium, but the annual cost of insurance is much less than the cost of a catastrophic health emergency. For low-income individuals, government subsidies can help pay monthly premiums. Most companies offer different plans, with different prices, that provide different groups of services. Buyers can choose the plan best suited to their needs and ability to pay.

PREVENTIVE SERVICES

Available preventive services vary according to age, gender, genetics, and medical history. They also vary according to the state and the particular health insurance plan. Specific preventive services are available for each age group. Newborns are screened for hearing disorders, sickle cell disease, hypothyroidism, and phenylketonuria (PKU). They are also given eye drops to prevent infections. Children and teens are screened for behavioral issues; blood pressure; height, weight, and body mass index; vision; obesity; and tuberculosis. Immunizations are a vital part of preventive services. Most are given in early childhood, but some are given later. For example, vaccination for human papillomavirus (HPV), which protects against reproductive system cancers, is recommended for children ages eleven or twelve and adolescents, according to the Centers for Disease Control and Prevention. Screenings primarily aimed at teenagers include screenings for depression, hepatitis B, and HIV. Counseling for teens at high risk for sexually transmitted infections (STIs) is also available. Common preventive tests for adults include those for blood pressure, cholesterol, colorectal cancer, depression, diabetes (Type 2), obesity, HIV, and diseases related tobacco use. Screenings available for women include breast cancer, cervical cancer, and domestic violence (including counseling).

Finally, since signing of the Affordable Care Act (ACA) in 2010, the government requires health insurance coverage. At first, those without it had to pay a yearly penalty. But, beginning in 2019, the fee for being uninsured was reduced to zero in most states, according to ObamaCareFacts.com. But with or without a penalty, there is much to be said for the benefits and peace of mind that come with having health insurance.

WHAT HEALTH INSURANCE COVERS

Health insurance plans vary not only in cost, but in what services the policy covers. Policies should be chosen to meet each person's health needs. The ACA requires that any health insurance policy must cover ten essential health benefits (EHBs). These include outpatient care, emergency services, and hospitalization, including surgery. They include maternity and newborn care, and pediatric (child) care. They include prescription drugs and care for mental health and substance abuse disorders, including psychotherapy and counseling. They include laboratory services and rehabilitative services and devices for people with injuries, disabilities, or chronic conditions. Finally, they include preventive and wellness services and management of chronic diseases. In addition to these EHBs, more expensive health insurance plans may cover other more specific and more expensive types of care. Most policies also cover a set of preventive services.

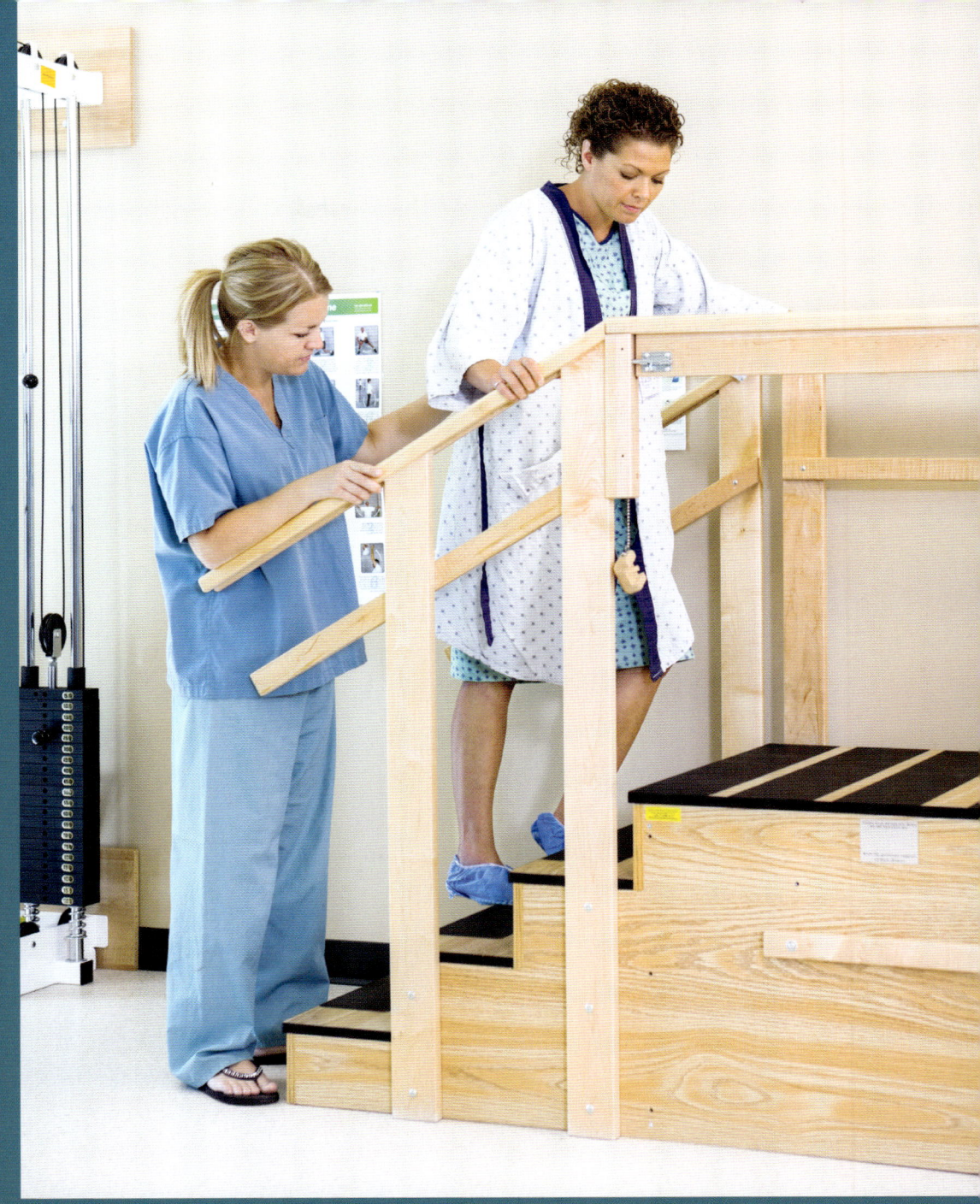

Health insurance covers a variety of services. One of these may be rehabilitative services. This patient is receiving physical therapy after an injury.

WHO NEEDS HEALTH INSURANCE?

Health care plans typically have a list of prescription medications that they will cover. These medications will be less expensive than those not on the list. Sometimes, individuals buy a separate plan to cover prescriptions. The choice of prescription coverage depends on the individual's needs and their ability to pay.

When considering medical care, it is important to distinguish between medical necessities and medical benefits. A medical necessity is a treatment that a doctor considers essential. It may or may not be covered by the person's health insurance. A medical benefit is a service that is covered by the insurer. Insurance companies determine which tests, drugs, and services they will cover. They base these decisions on the types of medical care needed by most patients. This approach means that, if a doctor prescribes a service that is unusual or not typical of most patients, the insurance company may refuse to cover it, even if the doctor considers it necessary. The patient would then have to cover the cost.

MYTHS & FACTS

MYTH **You don't receive any health care services until you pay your deductible.**

Fact *Although you must pay the deductible before insurance pays for many services, some preventive services, such as vaccinations, are available at any time.*

MYTH **Most health insurance premiums are unaffordable.**

Fact *Premiums vary in cost. Low-income individuals or families may qualify for subsidies under the Affordable Care Act or may qualify for Medicaid.*

MYTH **All plans offered by a given insurance provider are the same.**

Fact *Insurance providers usually have a variety of plans, with varying costs and varying services.*

CHAPTER TWO

TYPES OF HEALTH INSURANCE

Health care in the United States comes in many forms. Many people are insured through group plans provided by their employers. Low-income individuals are insured through the government program Medicaid; those sixty-five and older qualify for Medicare, another government program. Some individuals and families have private insurance. In March 2010, the US Congress passed the Affordable Care Act, or ACA (nicknamed Obamacare), which was designed to make affordable health insurance available to more people, partly by expanding Medicaid coverage. There are also temporary and supplementary insurance plans used in special circumstances.

GROUP HEALTH INSURANCE

Group health insurance is obtained through an employer. It is purchased by the employer and offered to all eligible employees, usually those working full-time, although part-time employees may also be covered. The coverage can also be extended to families (dependents) of eligible employees. Employees and family members cannot be denied coverage if they have an existing or preexisting medical condition. Usually a premium is deducted from the employee's paycheck each month, but the employer absorbs some or most of the cost. Group health insurance is used by companies of all sizes. It is significantly less expensive than individual coverage, because the risk is spread over more people. Larger businesses typically charge less and provide more extensive coverage.

Group coverage uses health insurance provider networks to offer discounted health care. The provider network is a group of

Group health insurance is less expensive than individual insurance because it is purchased (usually by an employer) through large companies able to insure many people and spread the risk.

TYPES OF HEALTH INSURANCE

medical suppliers, including primary care physicians, specialist physicians, labs, X-ray facilities, home health care providers, medical equipment providers, same-day surgery centers, and others. Health insurance companies expect insured individuals to use the providers in their network. All providers have met the plan's quality standards and have agreed to accept a discounted price for their services because being in the network assures them of more patients. If the insured prefers to use an out-of-network provider, he or she will pay considerably more—possibly the entire cost of the service.

There are several different forms of group health insurance. One of the most common is the HMO, or health maintenance organization. Members of an HMO are required to select a primary care physician (PCP) from the list of in-service providers. The PCP may refer the patient to in-service specialists as needed. Out-of-network services are usually only covered in emergencies. PPOs, or preferred provider organizations, give the insured more leeway. The insured may choose a PCP from outside the network, but the plan will cover these services at a lower level than in-service providers.

Two types of group plans, the EPO and the POS, combine aspects of both HMOs and PPOs. In an EPO, or exclusive provider organization, the insured does not have to choose a PCP, but is not allowed to seek coverage outside the network. In a POS, or point of service, plan, the insured must designate a PCP, who will then make referrals to in-service specialists. But, as in a PPO, the insured can use out-of-service providers, if they assume the greater cost.

Health Insurance Plan Types

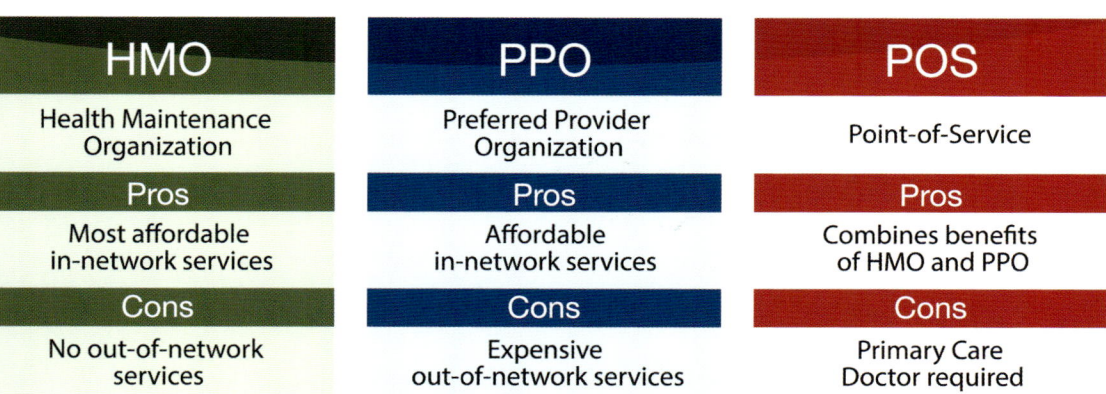

Various types of health insurance plans are available, including HMO, PPO, and POS plans. People should research each type of plan and determine which one best meets their needs.

They may also have to pay for deductibles and other out-of-pocket expenses.

Employer-funded group health insurance is lost when the insured leaves the job. A COBRA (Consolidated Omnibus Budget Reconciliation Act) plan enables the insured to keep job-based insurance for up to eighteen months after the job ends. However, the employer no longer contributes; the insured must pay the entire cost. COBRA is a stopgap measure to ensure health coverage between jobs. It was once the only choice; now people can find other insurance through their state marketplace.

TYPES OF HEALTH INSURANCE

CONSUMER-DRIVEN HEALTH PLANS

Consumer-driven health plans (CDHPs) were devised in the early 2000s as an alternative to traditional employer-paid group health care. CDHPs were meant to decrease employer costs, increase employee access to insurance, and help employees make smarter health care decisions. These health care plans have low premiums, high deductibles, and tax-exempt savings accounts. CDHPs are good alternatives if properly used. They do save money for employers, which can mean success instead of failure for some small businesses. Employees spend less on unnecessary care. CDHPs save money for employees who rarely get sick; the money in their health savings accounts is theirs to spend. But, employees with CDHPs who have serious health problems end up paying most of the cost of their health care, which insurance would otherwise cover. It was intended that CDHPs would encourage employees to shop around for the most efficient care. However, many employees lack the education to distinguish between necessary and unnecessary care, and to find accurate information on the cost and quality of health care options. Proper education could overcome these difficulties.

MEDICAID AND CHIP

Government-sponsored health plans include Medicaid, the Children's Health Insurance Program (CHIP) coverage, and Medicare. Medicare is an insurance program; Medicaid and CHIP are not—they are assistance programs. Medicaid provides free or low-cost health coverage to low-income individuals and families, pregnant women, people who are elderly, and people who are disabled. Most health care is free. Sometimes, a small co-payment is required. Since the passage of the ACA, some states have expanded their Medicaid coverage to cover everyone below a specific income level. Medicaid is run cooperatively by the state and federal governments. There are federal Medicaid guidelines, but state rules vary.

CHIP is also an assistance program. It provides health care to children up to age nineteen whose family income is too

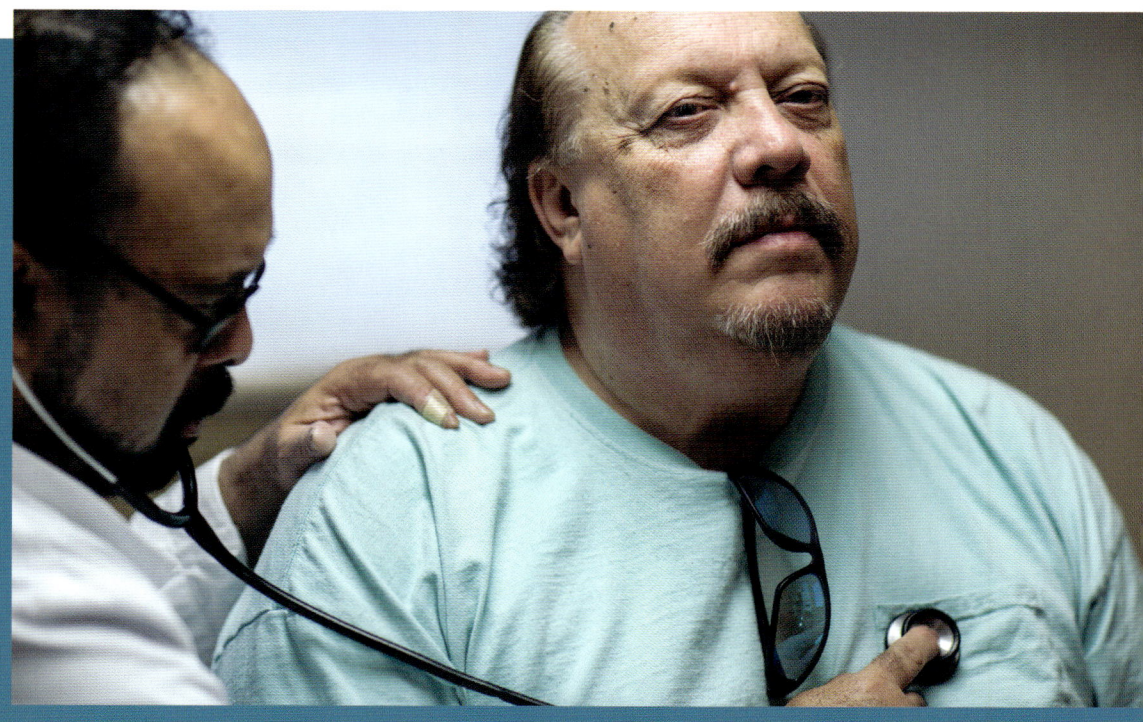

A doctor examines a Medicaid patient at the Heart City Health Center in Elkhart, Indiana. The doctor and patient are participating in the Healthy Indiana Plan (HIP).

TYPES OF HEALTH INSURANCE

high to qualify for Medicaid. The income level is set by each state. In forty-six states and the District of Columbia, children whose family incomes are 200 percent above the Federal Poverty Level (FPL) are eligible; in a few states, the cutoff is 300 percent above the FPL. In addition to those eligible because of income, children of public employees and children and pregnant women who are lawful US residents are eligible for CHIP coverage. It also covers prenatal care for pregnant women. CHIP is available either through Medicaid or through separate CHIP programs. Individual states administer the CHIP program, and it is funded jointly by the state and federal governments.

MEDICARE

Medicare is a federal insurance program. It is the same throughout the country; it does not vary by

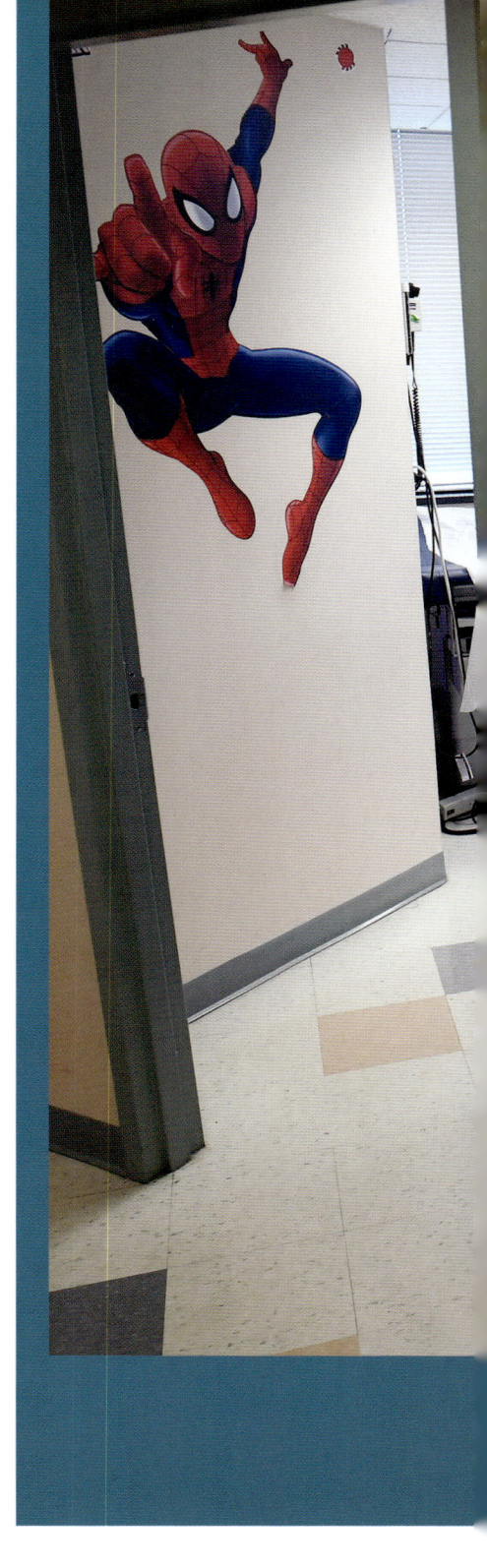

The CHIP program provides aid for children in low-income families. Here, a mother and baby see a doctor for a check-up at INOVA Cares Clinic for Children in Falls Church, Virginia.

TYPES OF HEALTH INSURANCE

state. It is run by a federal agency, the Centers for Medicare & Medicaid Services. Covered individuals have paid into trust funds, and their medical bills are paid from this fund. People become eligible for Medicare at age sixty-five, regardless of income. It also serves younger people who are disabled or on dialysis. Medicare patients pay deductibles and a few other costs. They pay small monthly premiums (taken out of Social Security checks) for nonhospital coverage. Medicare Part A is hospital insurance. It covers stays at hospitals, skilled nursing facilities, and hospices, as well as home health care,

SAVED BY MEDICAID

Alison Chandra's son was born with a rare congenital deformity known as heterotaxy syndrome. In this condition, the child's internal organs are located in abnormal positions within the body cavity. He required four open-chest surgeries before he was three years old. Because of their low income, the Chandra family was covered by Medicaid, which paid for prenatal care and their son's first two surgeries. One of these surgeries required ten hours in the operating room, one week in the cardiac intensive care unit, and one week on the cardiac floor. The total cost was $231,115, but after Medicaid, the Chandras owed only $500. Now, the family is covered by insurance through the father's new employer. But without Medicaid, they, like many other Americans, might have had to file for bankruptcy.

lab tests, and surgery. Medicare Part B is medical insurance. It covers health care provider services (for example, doctor visits), outpatient care, durable medical equipment (such as wheelchairs), home health care, and some preventive services.

Additional Medicare health plans include Medicare Advantage plans and Medicare Medical Savings Accounts. Medicare Advantage plans cover all original Medicare services, and may cover extras, including dental, vision, hearing, and sometimes health and wellness programs. Most include prescription drug coverage (called Medicare Part D). They can choose not to cover services not considered medically necessary by Medicare. Usually, a person insured by a Medicare Advantage plan must pay a premium in addition to the Part B premium. Medicare Medical Savings Account (MSA) plans cover services similar to those covered by Medicare Advantage plans. An MSA combines a high-deductible Medicare Advantage Plan (Medicare Part C) with an MSA. This MSA is a special savings account that can be used to pay health care costs before the person meets the high deductible. The MSA plan deposits money into the person's account for this purpose.

Individuals who are disabled can apply for Social Security Disability Insurance. They must have worked and paid Social Security taxes for a certain length of time to qualify. They must also have medical issues that meet the Social Security Administration's definition of disability. Another program for those who are disabled is Supplemental Security Income, which determines benefits based on financial need.

INDIVIDUAL AND FAMILY HEALTH INSURANCE

Since 2014, when the ACA's main parts went into effect, individuals purchasing health insurance usually go through a health insurance marketplace, also known as a health exchange. Each state has a health exchange, and services vary by state. The marketplace enables people to compare

Mayer Kotlarsky, owner of the Village Pharmacy in Deerfield Beach, Florida, answers questions for a Medicare patient. Prescriptions are covered under Medicare Part D.

insurance plans, learn more about health insurance, find out if they are eligible for tax credits or specific programs, and enroll in the health care plan of their choice. Every year, the marketplace has an open enrollment period. During this time, people can apply for subsidies, switch plans, or enroll in a new plan. Although no one is required to use their state marketplace, it is open to everyone and is often the easiest way to choose a health care plan.

Three types of individual health care plans meet ACA standards. These include major medical plans, qualified health plans, and catastrophic plans. Major medical plans are those available without a subsidy. They are meant for people who do not want or do not qualify for a subsidy. They help people avoid paying a tax penalty, and they meet all the coverage required by the ACA. Qualified health plans are typically meant for those who do qualify for subsidies, although they can also be used without subsidies. They can be purchased through either private insurance companies or through a state-sponsored health insurance exchange.

Catastrophic plans are available only to people under the age of thirty and do not qualify for government subsidies. They prevent the person from owing a penalty for being uninsured. They have lower premiums, but very high deductibles. They provide essential, but minimal, coverage, which usually does not include prescription drugs or shots. These plans often act as safety nets for people who cannot afford thorough coverage, but who want protection in case of accidents and serious illness.

The many forms of insurance available in the United States make selecting an insurance plan difficult. But the first step is knowing what is available. The second is considering what factors—such as age, health, lifestyle, and marital status—should enter into making decisions about a health care plan. The third is determining which type of plan—group, government, or private—is most appropriate for your needs. This procedure is an ongoing process; individuals' needs change as they go through life, as do health care types and availability.

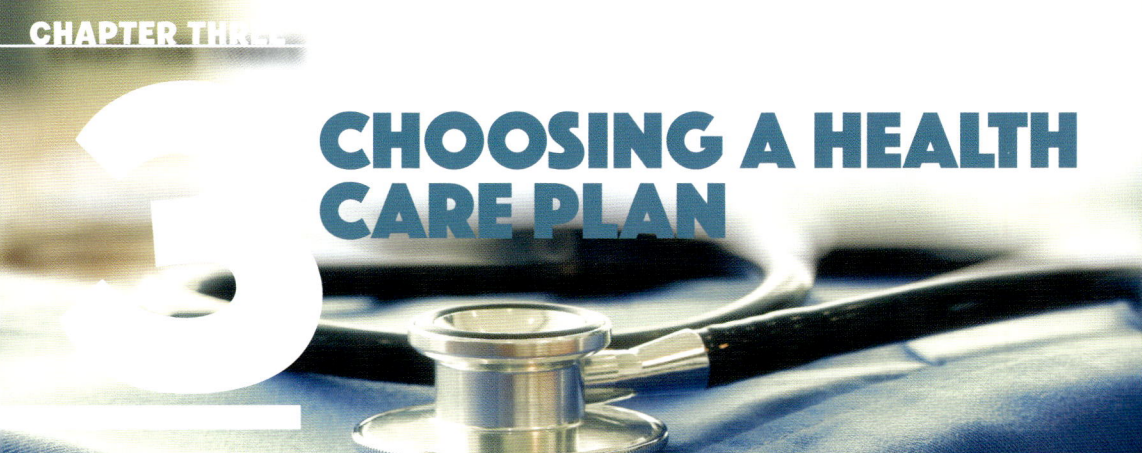

CHAPTER THREE
CHOOSING A HEALTH CARE PLAN

Choosing a health insurance plan is like negotiating a maze. There are so many directions to go, so many wrong turns to take. Only one path results in the best plan—the plan the shopper can afford and that meets all of his or her needs. Cost is likely the most important factor; if shoppers can't pay the premiums, the insurance won't help them. But other factors are important, too. Insurance needs change drastically with a person's age and life stage. The insurance needs of a young, healthy person are different from those of an elderly person with Alzheimer's disease. The needs of a college student are different from those of a young, married couple expecting a child. Each person must consider his or her own health and lifestyle needs, and choose an insurance plan that meets them.

QUESTIONS TO ASK

When shopping for health insurance, it pays to ask and answer a number of questions about one's own health needs. An employed person should ask if the employer's insurance

During the open enrollment period, people can enroll in or change their health insurance coverage without restrictions. Here, a woman signs up for ACA coverage in Miami, Florida.

plan is really the best fit. A healthy person paying for job-based insurance might do better buying individual insurance. Because job-based insurance rates are based on the average health of all enrollees, its premiums might be higher than premiums for individual insurance for a healthy person. Also, when figuring the cost of insurance, it is important to consider more than just the premium cost. Out-of-pocket expenses may be so high that they outweigh the savings from a low premium. Shoppers must ask whether they would rather pay high premiums or risk paying higher out-of-pocket expenses if they get sick or injured. They must strike a balance to get the best coverage.

Insurance companies may offer similar plans for different rates, so it is also important to shop around. This point is important when first enrolling for insurance, but it is also important to check the competition every year, during the open enrollment period of the state's marketplace. According to eHealthInsurance.com, seven of every ten people can save money on health insurance by shopping around.

Savvy health insurance shoppers should check that their chosen plan covers their preferred doctor. This investigation means both checking the insurance website and calling the doctor's billing office, as the website may be out of date. Also, be sure the chosen plan covers prescription drugs. Government subsidies can be very helpful for people with low incomes, but shoppers must understand how they work. Subsidy amounts are based on yearly income, but an insured person who makes more than the estimated income during the year may later have to pay back some of it. Some people may want to buy supplemental insurance for extra protection against specific types of health emergencies, such as cancer. Finally, after a person signs up for an insurance policy, there may be a period of up to six weeks before the policy goes into effect. During this time, the person may buy short-term insurance to be protected against unexpected health emergencies.

INSURANCE COSTS AND METAL LEVELS

In the health insurance marketplace, a shopper can choose a health care plan in one of four "metal levels"—bronze, silver, gold, or platinum. Metal levels are not based on quality of care,

FALLING THROUGH THE CRACKS: THE UNINSURED

Multiple sclerosis (MS) is a progressive nervous system disease that disrupts signals to and from the brain. It causes unpredictable symptoms, including paralysis. Alicia is uninsured. MS has confined her to a wheelchair, she cannot leave her home, and she cannot afford home care. Her two children, ages ten and twelve, take care of her. According to the Kaiser Family Foundation, in 2013, just before the Affordable Care Act went into effect, more than forty-four million people, like Alicia, were uninsured. By 2016, the number of uninsured had declined to 26.7 million; it rose to 27.4 million in 2017. Forty-five percent of uninsured adults blame the high cost of insurance for their uninsured state. Others lack coverage through a job. The Medicaid option is not available to all. The ACA expanded Medicaid coverage to non-elderly adults, but each state must choose to expand coverage. Individuals in states that choose not to expand coverage often remain without health care. Others are unaware that they might be eligible for financial assistance (subsidies) through the ACA, and also remain uninsured. Most uninsured are members of low-income families, with at least one working family member. Adults are more likely to be uninsured than children, and people of color are more likely than whites not of Hispanic or Latino origin to be uninsured.

but on how the average cost of insurance is shared between the insurance company and the insured. In a bronze plan, the insured pays approximately 40 percent and the insurance company the other 60 percent. In a silver plan, the percentages are 30 percent for the insured and 70 percent for the insurance company. In a gold plan, the insured pays 20 percent, the insurance company 80 percent. And in a platinum plan, the insured pays 10 percent, the insurance company 90 percent.

Preventive health care is vital to remain healthy and is covered by most health care plans. Here, a doctor uses a stethoscope to check a young man's heartbeat.

The shared percentages include premiums, deductibles, co-payments, coinsurance, and out-of-pocket expenses. All plans provide preventive care, and some offer discounted services before the deductible is met.

Bronze plans have the lowest monthly premiums, but the highest cost when the insured needs health care. As you progress through silver, gold, and platinum, premiums rise and the amount the insured pays for health care drops. Bronze plans are good for people who are generally healthy but want to protect themselves against catastrophic injuries or illnesses. They require the insured to pay for most routine care. Silver plans have moderate monthly premiums and moderate costs for care. They enable the insured to pay slightly less for routine care. A gold plan could be the best value if you use a lot of health care. A platinum plan would be even better, if the insured can pay the higher premium.

About 70 percent of ACA enrollees chose silver plans, according to Colleen McGuire, writing for HealthCare.com. Silver plans tend to strike the best balance between affordable monthly premiums and an affordable deductible. Also, some families qualify for cost-sharing subsidies, in which the government pays part of the insurance costs. To take advantage of these subsidies, insurance shoppers must choose a silver plan.

INSURANCE FOR YOUNG PEOPLE

Most young people are healthy, and many assume they don't need health insurance. Often, they are transitioning from student life to working life, they have low incomes, and therefore they avoid getting health insurance because they cannot afford the premiums (or assume they cannot). But even young healthy people have health concerns. According to Jenifer Dorsey, writing for Health eDeals, the most common reasons for twenty-somethings to be hospitalized include pregnancy, mental health issues, and injuries or poisoning. Health coverage helps young people avoid the high costs associated with these and other emergencies.

People in their twenties have a variety of options. Students may be covered by student health plans or their parents' insurance. Those with very low incomes may seek Medicaid coverage; those starting jobs may be covered by employer-paid insurance plans. Others may choose to apply for their own individual major medical plans. These plans meet ACA guidelines and may also include catastrophic plans and subsidies.

Student health plans can be an easy and affordable option for college students. Usually, student health plans are qualifying plans; that is, they meet the requirements of the ACA. If the student's college lacks health coverage, or a student lives in the same state as his or her parents and is under age twenty-six, he or she can be covered under the parents' plan. A student who attends college out of state may also be able to stay on the parents' plan, depending on the rules of the individual plan. Students with or without student health coverage can also apply for health insurance themselves, through the health insurance marketplace. If a student is not claimed as a dependent by parents or anyone else, that student must apply for his or her own health coverage. Applications can be made directly to an insurance company or through the marketplace.

Often, short-term, or temporary, insurance is an excellent option for young people. Short-term plans last between 30 and 364 days, depending on the state. They provide catastrophic coverage for unexpected health conditions. Benefits include things such as ambulance services, surgery, hospital room and board, emergency room treatment, and intensive care. Short-term insurance coverage is useful in circumstances when young people are between insurance plans, including when they cannot be covered by their parents or they reach age twenty-six and must be removed from the parents' plan. It may include people transitioning between jobs or those between school and a first job.

Short-term plans have both advantages and disadvantages. They become active immediately, often by the next day after enrollment. The insured can choose his or her own health care provider. However, they do not include the ten EHBs

Students can be covered under student health plans or under their parents' health plan. Coverage is important for prevention, unexpected illness, and protection against injury for students in sports.

required by the ACA. They can deny or exclude coverage for preexisting conditions or for benefits such as prescription drugs. They may limit the amount paid for hospital stays or surgeries, and they may not cover 100 percent of some preventive services.

The catastrophic coverage provided by short-term insurance is a special kind of insurance available only to people under the age of thirty, or to those who can get a "hardship exemption" stating that they are unable to afford health insurance. These plans meet all requirements of qualified health plans under the ACA, but they cover very few benefits other than for catastrophic health emergencies—that is, they cover little routine care. They have low premiums but higher out-of-pocket costs.

INSURANCE FOR PEOPLE WHO ARE SELF-EMPLOYED

A self-employed person makes money but has no employees. Examples are freelancers, consultants, independent contractors, and entrepreneurs. With no outside employer, these people are ineligible for most group insurance. One option is a group insurance plan through a trade association in the self-employed person's field, such as the Writers Guild of America or the Actors' Equity Association. However, there is a fee for joining any association; a large fee may be greater than the health benefit you receive.

Another option is a new category of health care known as health cost sharing. It is meant for generally healthy people to protect themselves against health emergencies. The person must be in good health and must agree to live by a specified code of healthy living to be accepted. The cost is only a few hundred dollars per year, and the program provides no-frills health care. A third option is a professional employer organization (PEO), a type of company that outsources management tasks such as

Self-employed people, such as freelancers or this young entrepreneur, may find it difficult to afford health insurance. They may get insurance through nontraditional routes, such as health cost sharing plans.

accounting and payroll for employers. Self-employed workers and entrepreneurs who sign up with PEOs are eligible for their health care plans.

Many people, especially adults who are not elderly, can usually obtain insurance through standard methods, such as the state marketplaces and employer-based insurance. However, those in special groups, such as the young and the self-employed, may need to seek out nontraditional approaches. Somewhere, there is a health care solution for everyone, but these solutions are not always easy to ferret out.

CHAPTER 4: SUPPLEMENTING HEALTH INSURANCE

The types of health insurance coverage available depend on a person's age and life situation. These include government insurance such as Medicare, group insurance such as that provided by an employer, or individual private insurance, obtained either on one's own or through an ACA state marketplace. But sometimes, additional insurance is needed to cover services not included in ordinary policies or to cover an insured with greater-than-average needs. These supplementary insurance policies are separate from traditional policies. They include policies for vision and dental coverage, for special types of medical issues, and for long-term care, including mental health care.

SUPPLEMENTAL POLICIES

Supplemental insurance is extra insurance meant to pay for services and expenses not covered by regular insurance. It is purchased in addition to regular insurance. Television watchers are probably familiar with the Aflac duck, the symbol for the largest US company providing supplemental insurance.

OBAMACARE VERSUS TRUMPCARE

Obamacare is a nickname for the health care reform law proposed by President Barack Obama and signed into law on March 23, 2010. This law, the Patient Protection and Affordable Care Act (PPACA), is usually called the Affordable Care Act, or ACA. Its goal is to provide affordable health insurance to more Americans, improve health care and insurance quality, regulate the industry, and reduce the cost of US health care. The ACA set up health insurance marketplaces in all states, expanded Medicaid in all states that agreed, and expanded employer coverage. It guaranteed coverage for people with preexisting conditions, allowed young people to stay on their parents' policies until age twenty-six, and provided low-cost insurance coverage for twenty million previously uninsured people. Republicans in Congress considered the ACA a form of socialized medicine and tried to repeal it, unsuccessfully. But they have changed many of its provisions to make the law less effective. The changes, called the American Health Care Act of 2017, have become known as Trumpcare. One change, removal of the penalty for not having insurance, means many healthy people will not get insurance, and premiums will rise. According to Michael Hiltzik in the *Los Angeles Times*, the projected premium increases in California for 2019 are in the range of 16 to 30 percent.

Services paid for by supplemental policies vary with the policy. Some pay for out-of-pocket expenses, such as deductibles and co-payments. Others pay cash, either as a lump sum or on a regular basis. The cash covers expenses related to the person's medical condition, such as lost wages, transportation to medical facilities, food, medication, or other items.

Many people have major medical plans and do not need supplemental insurance. Some individuals and families fill

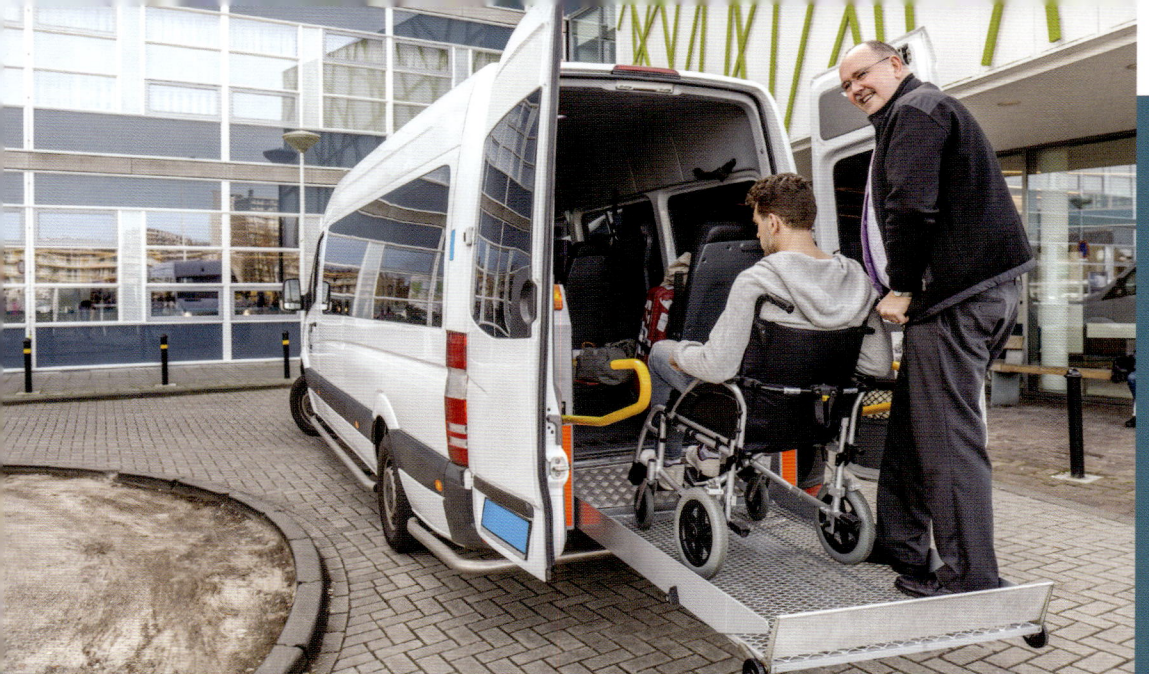

Some medical expenses, such as transportation to medical appointments for wheelchair-bound patients, are not covered by health insurance. They require supplemental insurance.

gaps in their health coverage using short-term health plans or supplemental fixed benefit, or fixed indemnity, health plans. These plans do not conform to the ACA. They pay out a fixed amount if the insured suffers a specific injury or illness not covered by their regular health insurance plan. They may only cover a specific set of injuries, illnesses, drugs, or services, and may not cover hospital costs. Each person must be careful that the fixed benefit covers that individual's specific needs. Other people may buy supplemental plans specifically for dental or vision coverage, which are not part of most medical policies. Usually, families benefit most from dental or vision plans.

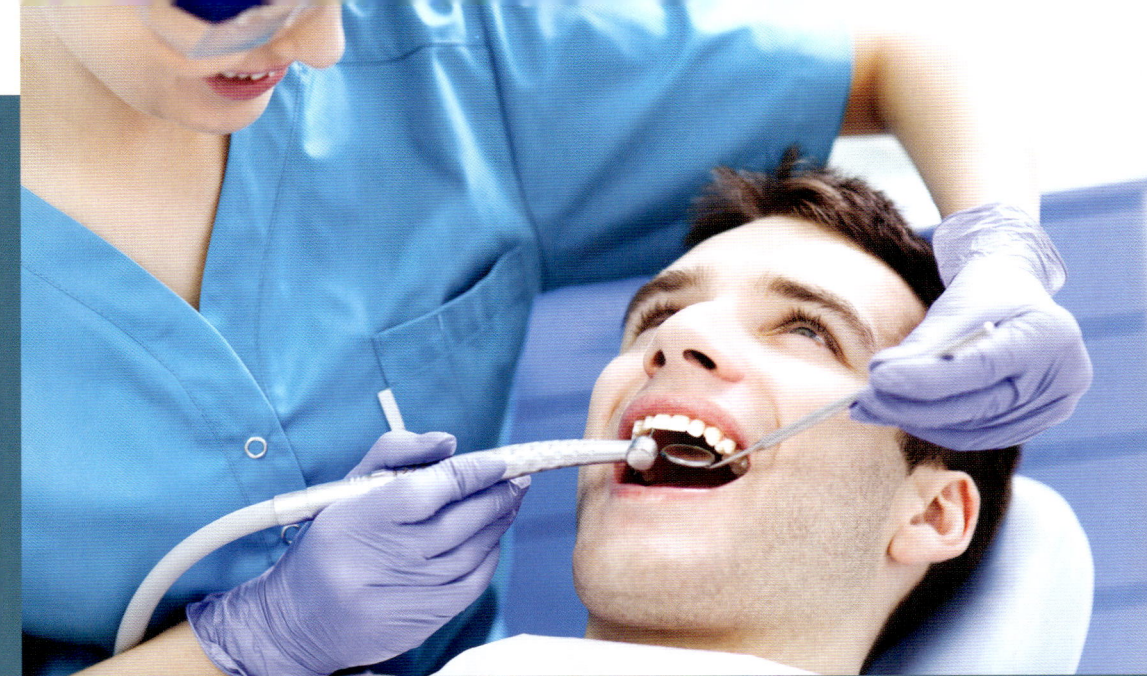

An important benefit of supplemental insurance is paying for dental care, shown here, or vision care. Many basic medical plans do not cover these needs.

    Three types of supplemental insurance are common in the United States. One type is critical illness insurance, or disease-specific insurance. The most common type is a cancer policy; heart disease policies are also purchased frequently. These policies usually pay a lump-sum benefit that covers illness-related expenditures, such as deductibles, out-of-network specialists, travel and lodging for treatment away from home, experimental treatments, child care and household assistance, or regular living expenses. The expenses covered vary by policy.

    A second type of supplemental insurance is the accidental death policy. There are two types: accidental death and dismemberment (AD&D) and accident health insurance. They

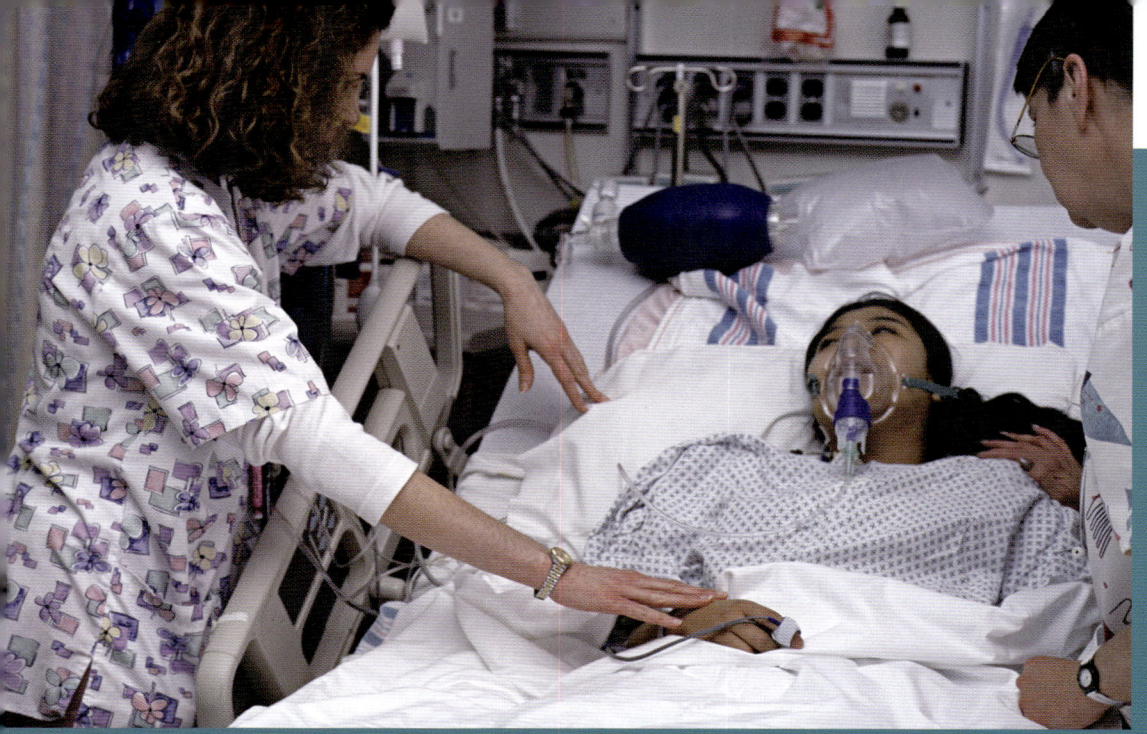

A nurse cares for a fifteen-year-old patient who has had heart surgery. For extended hospital stays like this one, indemnity insurance can be valuable.

are often sold together. An AD&D policy pays a lump sum to the beneficiary of a person killed in an accident. Smaller amounts may be paid if the person lost an eye or limb, or suffered paralysis. Accident health insurance is often purchased by healthy people who have high-deductible policies. In the event of a major accident, the policy will help them cover the deductible and other extra expenses. The third type is hospital indemnity insurance, also known as hospital confinement insurance. In case of an extended hospital stay, this policy will help defray costs not covered by a regular insurance policy. It may only kick in after a waiting period.

Medicare has several types of supplement plans. The Medicare Supplement Insurance (Medigap) policy supplements Medicare Parts A and B. Private companies sell Medigap policies. Medigap is meant to "cover the gap" between what Medicare pays and the total cost of the insured's medical expenses. Medicare Advantage is not technically a Medicare supplement plan, but it contains plans that do supplement typical Medicare coverage. An insured cannot have both Medigap coverage and a Medicare Advantage plan. Medicare Part D prescription drug coverage is another gap plan that pays prescription drug costs not covered by other insurance. It can be used with Medigap and is usually included as part of Medicare Advantage plans.

LONG-TERM CARE INSURANCE

Sometimes people need long-term care; that is, they need help for weeks, months, or even years doing everyday activities such as bathing, dressing, and feeding themselves, as well as skilled medical care. People needing long-term care may be elderly or they may have chronic illnesses or disabilities that prevent them from caring for themselves.

According to AARP (American Association of Retired Persons), about half of Americans over age sixty-five will eventually need long-term care (LTC) and will spend an average of $140,000 per person. But relatively few Americans have LTC insurance, which covers services not covered by Medicare, including nursing home, assisted-living, and in-home care. For some time, people bought traditional LTC policies, which involved paying an annual premium in exchange for financial assistance when the insured needed day-to-day care. In 2018, an LTC policy paid a daily stipend of about $160, and the annual premium was approximately $2,700. But insurers have been less than accurate in forecasting the payouts for which they will be responsible. In the 1990s, more than 100 companies sold LTC insurance; by 2018, there were fewer than fifteen. AARP suggests that not everyone needs to buy LTC insurance, but everyone does need a plan. Some people might rely on retirement savings; those with low incomes might count on Medicaid. Still others might have nearby relatives who can help. A person or family who does have a high enough income to consider LTC insurance should try to buy it when they are relatively young and healthy—say, in their fifties, rather than their seventies.

LTC policies are available from the same sources as typical health care insurance. These sources include individual insurance companies, employer-based plans, professional or service organizations, or State Partnership Programs that cooperate with Medicaid. There are also joint policies, in which a single policy covers more than one adult—spouses or siblings, for example. Joint policies come with a risk. They usually have a maximum benefit that applies to everyone insured. If the benefit is $100,000 and one spouse uses $60,000 of the benefit, there will be only $40,000 left for the other, regardless of need.

LTC policies cover a variety of services and care in a variety of settings. These include nursing homes, assisted living, adult day care arrangements, home care, home modifications (such

Long-term care (LTC) insurance is becoming more important as people live longer. At some point, many elderly people begin to require assistance in their daily lives.

as installing wheelchair ramps), services by trained and licensed professionals, and sometimes future service options (the ability to add a service that is needed after the policy goes into effect). All policies exclude coverage for some conditions. The purchaser should read the policy carefully and be aware of these exclusions. They might include conditions such as Alzheimer's disease, heart disease, diabetes, or some forms of cancer.

There are now alternatives to traditional long-term care insurance. One of these is the hybrid plan that combines life insurance with long-term care insurance. It allows the insured to draw money from the life insurance benefit to pay for long-term care. Whatever remains becomes a death benefit for the insured's heirs. Another option is a short-term care policy that lasts from three months to one year and pays for the same types of care as an LTC policy.

Sometimes people require hospital treatment for mental health conditions such as depression or anxiety. Typical medical insurance policies often have some mental health coverage. All policies purchased after January 1, 2014, when the ACA went into effect, are required to include mental health coverage as

Mental health coverage, including visits to a therapist for depression or anxiety, are more often covered by health care plans than in the past. ACA plans require this coverage.

one of their essential health benefits, or EHBs. Medicare and Medicaid both offer inpatient mental health coverage.

When considering the type of health insurance coverage that is needed, the shopper should think broadly. It is important to cover EHBs, and all the health concerns that people typically have. But, to be prepared for any health emergency, shoppers should also consider unlikely events—major accidents or illnesses, specific conditions, mental health concerns, and the like. If the person is at risk for one or more of these conditions—if their work or lifestyle includes dangerous activities or if they have a family history of mental illness, for example—health insurance plans can be tailored to cover these factors. In addition, shoppers should adjust the health coverage as they age, adding supplemental or LTC coverage when it becomes appropriate.

10 GREAT QUESTIONS

TO ASK A HEALTH INSURANCE EXPERT

1. Why should young, healthy people have health insurance?

2. What are preventive services and why should health insurance cover them?

3. What is the difference between Medicare and Medicaid?

4. What is a health insurance marketplace and how is it used?

5. Who is eligible for group insurance, and who should look for individual coverage?

6. How does the size of the deductible relate to the size of the insurance premium?

7. What questions should I ask when I am choosing a health care plan?

8. What are the major health insurance options for people who are thirty and younger?

9. What are supplementary health insurance plans and how are they used?

10. What is universal health care and how does it compare to US health care?

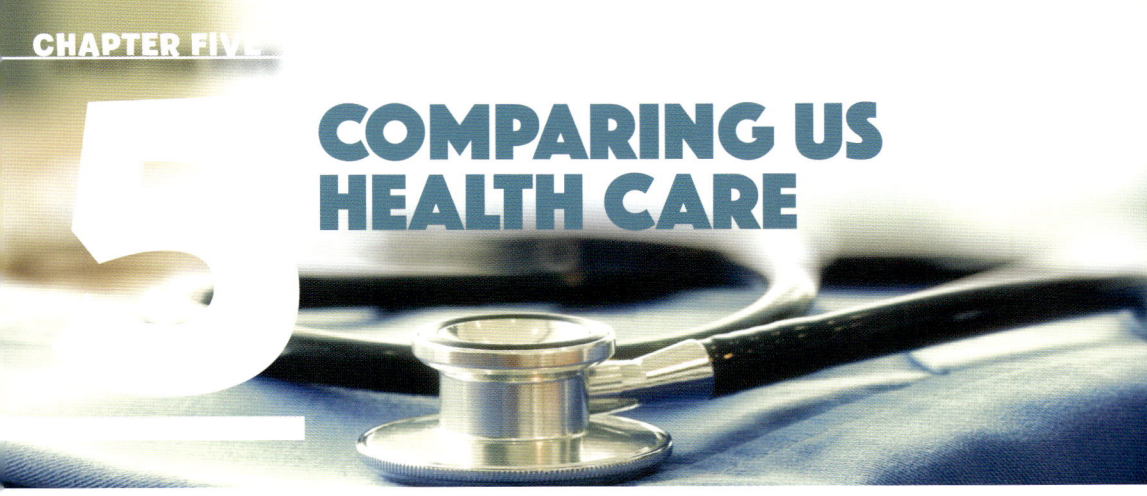

CHAPTER FIVE
COMPARING US HEALTH CARE

According to Kamal and Cox, writing for the Peterson-Kaiser Health System Tracker, the average US patient in 2016 spent $10,348 on health care per year. The average expenditure for eleven more of the world's wealthiest countries was $5,198, half the US cost. The per capita cost for these countries ranged between $7,919 for Switzerland (second only to the United States), and $4,192 for the United Kingdom.

Why are US health care prices so high? Many people think it is because of the excellence of US health care. But based on United Nations standards, the quality of US health care ranks twenty-eighth in the world—below almost all other rich nations, according to Annalisa Merelli, writing for Quartz. Some people blame the high prices on a high number of specialists, but the percentage of US specialists is comparable to the percentage in other countries. Others suggest that Americans use more services, but the United States has the second fewest doctor visits per year and the third-shortest hospital stays of the twelve countries in the Peterson-Kaiser study. Their data show that health care costs in the United States are simply higher than those in other countries. Drugs, doctors and other practitioners, diagnostic services, diagnostic tests, and administration all cost more. According to Yoni Blumberg, writing for CNBC, it is harder to obtain health care in the United States. Many people fail to seek health care because they cannot afford it. And all or nearly all people in other countries have access to health care, but 10 percent of the US population had no health care in 2016.

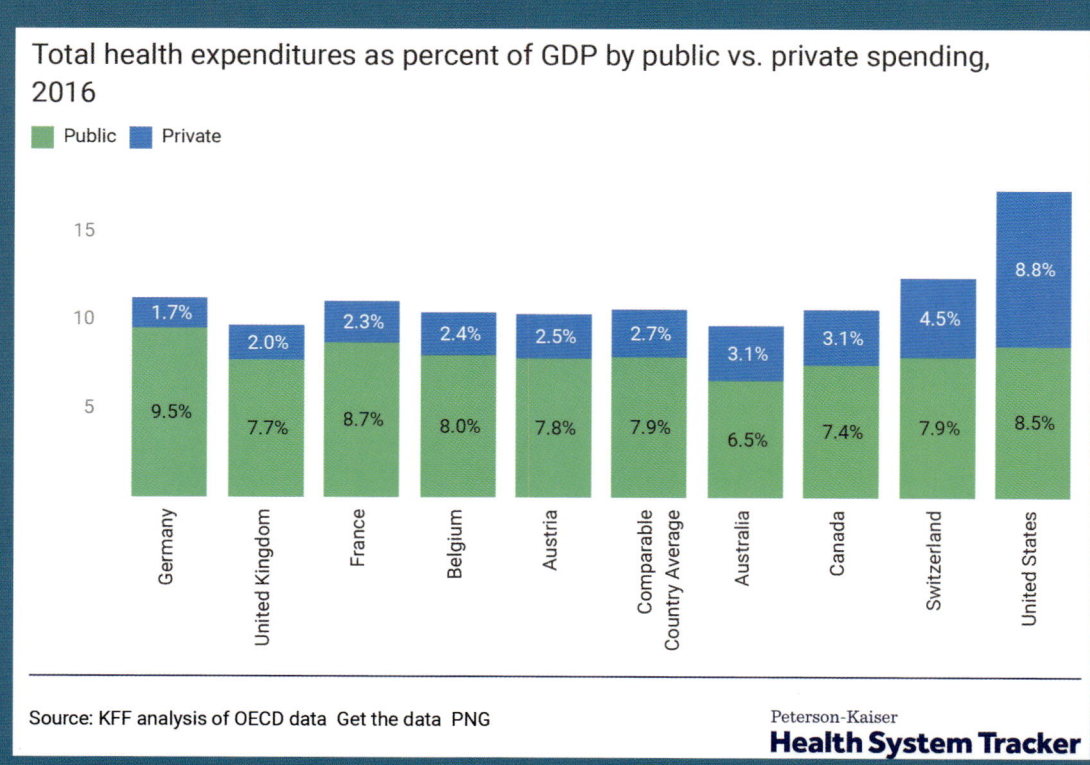

The percentage of public health care expenditures in the United States (8.5 percent) is similar to European percentages. But US health care in all areas is higher than in European countries.

HEALTH CARE OR HEALTH INSURANCE?

According to Dr. Katherine Baicker of Harvard's T. H. Chan School of Public Health, people want health outcomes, or better health, rather than health care. Health care is the process for getting better health outcomes. Most people would prefer less health care (and less health insurance). Edward D. Kleinbard, writing for *The Hill*, distinguishes between health care coverage and health insurance. Like Baicker, Kleinbard says Americans want a functional health coverage system, in which they receive all services necessary for life and good health at an affordable cost. The high cost of medical care, combined with the rise in health care costs with age, makes government subsidies necessary to provide functional health coverage for all. Medicare and Medicaid are examples. Tax-funded government payment is the model of health care for all developed countries except the United States. US health insurance markets are competitive and profit-based; therefore, they cannot support the health of *all* citizens—only those who can afford the insurance. Kleinbard concludes, "Health insurance is a luxury item for a few; reasonably priced health care services are what most Americans actually want."

UNIVERSAL COVERAGE OR SINGLE-PAYER?

Two terms are often used to describe health care coverage that ensures coverage to all members of a group, such as residents of a country. These terms, "universal health care" and " single-payer health care," are often used interchangeably, but they are not quite the same. Universal health care, or universal coverage, can mean two things. It can be a system in which every citizen can access health insurance, either public or private. Or, it can be a system in which every citizen has access to free or low-cost

Many Americans favor "Medicare for All," a single-payer system. Here, California demonstrators protest President Trump's attempted repeal of the ACA, which threatened to make health care less, not more, available.

basic services (such as prevention or emergency services) from a list of government-mandated standard benefits (EHBs).

In single-payer health care, the government authorizes and pays for all health benefits. There are no private insurance companies. Examples are Great Britain's and Canada's systems. In Great Britain, the National Health Service (NHS) controls access to health care services and employs doctors and other health care providers. Some progressive politicians, such as Vermont senator Bernie Sanders, have suggested that single-payer health care could be accomplished in the United States by providing "Medicare for All."

Some countries around the world, including Germany, the Netherlands, and Singapore, offer health care to all through public-private partnerships, rather than through single-payer health care. Singapore has been particularly successful with this type of system. It has extremely low infant mortality rates and long life expectancies.

FOR-PROFIT OR UNIVERSAL HEALTH CARE?

The high cost of health care in the United States means that millions of Americans lack access to medical care. This situation is partly because of the high cost of drugs and services and partly because health insurance is provided by private, for-profit insurance companies. The United States is the only industrialized nation that lacks universal health coverage—that is, it fails to provide all of its citizens with health care. According to Merelli, high costs and a lack of universal coverage are strongly connected. Universal health coverage is usually

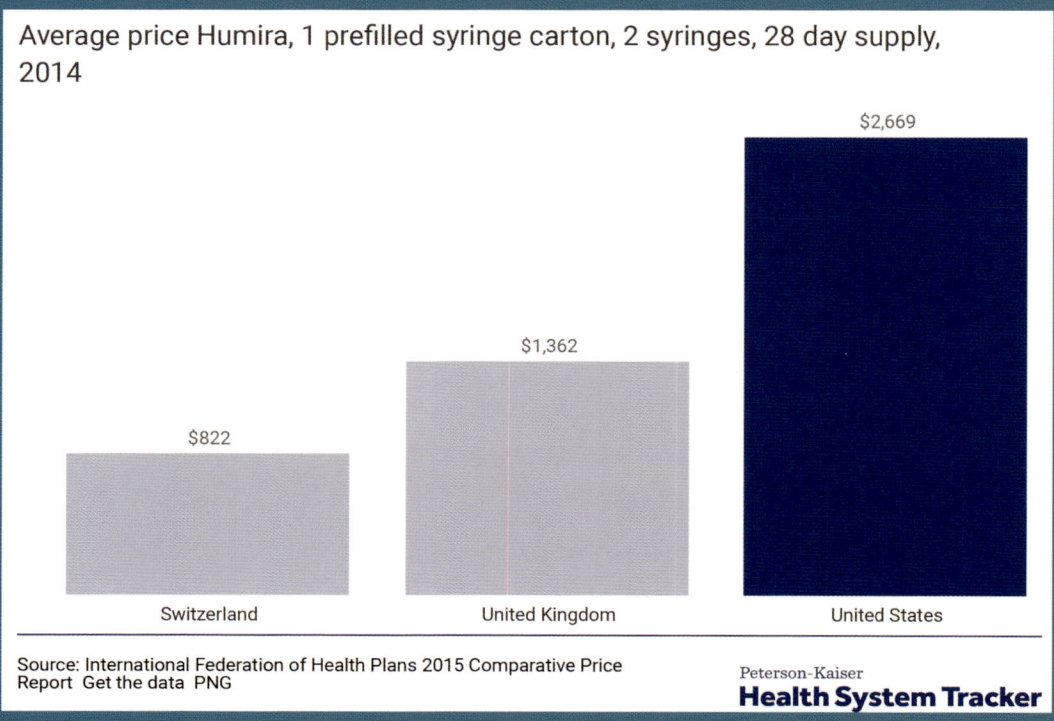

Humira is an immunosuppressive drug used to treat arthritis and other ailments. Its cost in the United States is double its cost in the United Kingdom and 3.25 times its cost in Switzerland.

carried out through single-payer health care; that is, the government pays health care costs through taxes. This factor keeps costs down because the government can regulate the prices of drugs and medical services and because it removes the need for high-priced private insurance companies.

Universal health care has other advantages. The standard of care applies to everyone—poor people are not denied access to new, high-priced treatments or technologies. Preventive care makes people healthier and cuts down on emergency room visits. But universal health care also has downsides. Healthy people must pay for the care of less healthy individuals. Chronic diseases such as diabetes and heart disease, which are most costly, can sometimes be prevented with healthy lifestyle choices, but people with guaranteed health care may be less likely to make these choices. Often, in universal systems, doctors might choose to spend less time with each patient to keep costs down, and people might have to wait for elective services. Finally, health care costs can overwhelm a country's budget, reducing funds for education and other programs.

Why does the United States not have universal coverage? Present-day health coverage resulted from a series of decisions, beginning early in the twentieth century. When government-funded health care or "socialized medicine" was first proposed, doctors, insurance companies, and businesses opposed it. They argued that it was the same as charity and that America was an individualistic, profit-based country with people that should not depend on government "handouts." They also associated it with communism, which was unpopular after the Bolshevik Revolution in the 1910s and completely out of favor after World War II, during the Cold War with the Soviet Union.

During World War II, after President Franklin Roosevelt froze labor wages, labor unions began negotiating to receive health benefits through employers, beginning the era of employer-sponsored health insurance. Several attempts to pass universal health care policies were made. In 1944, California proposed a plan for compulsory health insurance, paid for by Social Security. In 1949, President Harry Truman proposed a nationwide public health plan. In 1983, President Bill Clinton attempted a revision of the country's health care system, including universal health care. All of these attempts failed.

According to Theodore Brown, professor of public health and policy at the University of Rochester, and quoted by Annalisa Merelli in Quartz, hostility to universal health care because of its ties to communism or socialism is still strong. Most experts know that a single-payer health care system is necessary to enable broader coverage without higher costs. However, they consider it politically unfeasible. The United States lacks a Labor Party, or another party dedicated to the labor class, which would benefit most from universal health care. The health care problem is also tied to segregation and inequality. Minority populations are most likely to lack health care and health insurance. As of 2015, 12 percent of blacks and 17 percent of Hispanics were uninsured, compared to only 8 percent of whites, according to the Kaiser Family Foundation and quoted by Merelli.

HEALTH CARE IN OTHER COUNTRIES

All developed countries except the United States have some form of universal health care—that is, health care available to all citizens. Universal health care is expensive and uses a large percentage of the federal budget. It is usually funded by income taxes or general payroll taxes. How universal health care is accomplished varies by country. Most countries use government funds to pay for health care provided by private companies. Countries that pay this way include Canada, Australia, France, Germany, Switzerland, and Singapore.

The United States does this on a limited scale, with Medicare and Medicaid. Obamacare also provides government subsidies to health insurance companies to help low-income people afford insurance.

Socialized medicine is the form of health care in which the government both pays for and provides health care services. The United Kingdom's National Health Service (NHS) is an example of this type. Again, the United States has this sort of care in limited form: the Department of Veterans Affairs provides health care for the US armed forces.

In the United Kingdom, everyone can receive health care through the socialized medicine system known as the National Health Service (NHS). Here, a young patient receives a tuberculosis test.

Of the thirty-three developed countries, thirty-two have universal health care (the United States is the exception). These countries adopt one of three plans. First is the single-payer system, in which the government pays for health care by taxing its citizens. Twelve of the thirty-three countries, including Great Britain, follow this plan. Six of the countries require everyone to buy health insurance, either

UNIVERSAL HEALTH CARE IN GREAT BRITAIN

Erich McElroy, a comedian from Seattle, Washington, who has lived in London, England, for twenty years, tells a joke in his stand-up routine about his first visit to a British doctor. McElroy, quoted by Lauren Frayer of National Public Radio, says, "The doctor gave me a couple pills and sent me on my way." But he kept looking around for a place to pay. He finally went back to the receptionist and asked, "What do I do now?" She said, "You go home." The British audience laughs uproariously. Why? Because the idea of having to pay for health care in Great Britain is a foreign concept. People do pay at some point, through taxes. But no one is ever denied necessary health care, although they may have to wait for nonessential care, such as elective surgery. Because of the National Health Service, or NHS, all emergency care, surgery, radiation and chemotherapy, and other essential services are free. Medications are free or very inexpensive. The 2008 worldwide recession has put stress on the NHS, causing delays and cutting back services. But the British love their health care, and according to Frayer, "The NHS polls better than the queen."

through their employer or through the government. One example is Germany. Nine countries use a two-tier approach. The government taxes citizens to pay for basic health services, and citizens can buy private supplemental insurance to improve their level of care. France is the best example of this type.

Americans still have very mixed feelings about how health care should be paid for. Economist Jonathan Gruber of the Massachusetts Institute of Technology, quoted by Dana Connolly, writing for *The Hill*, sees universal care as inevitable. But, because equal health care is impossible, he foresees a two-tiered system, with a minimum standard of care covered by the government and supplemental care available through private insurance. Others are concerned that such a two-tier system will result in a health care system of "haves" and "have-nots," with the rich having unlimited care and the poor having the bare minimum.

The United States is in the midst of many health care changes. Tomorrow's young adults must pay attention to news about health care and keep up to date on the changes to health care laws. An understanding of the basics of health care and health insurance is vital to this process.

GLOSSARY

catastrophic coverage A type of health care plan generally available only to people under the age of thirty; it has low premiums but high out-of-pocket expenses and covers only catastrophic medical issues.

chronic A long-term illness or an illness that frequently recurs.

essential health benefits (EHBs) Health benefits that are considered essential and must be covered by health insurance policies; the ACA lists ten specific EHBs that policies must cover.

health insurance marketplace (health exchange) An organization in each state through which individuals can purchase health insurance that is standardized and satisfies ACA requirements.

insurance A form of financial protection bought by an individual or entity to protect against damage, loss, injury, or illness.

insurance claim A formal request from an insured person to an insurance company, requesting payment or compensation for damage, loss, injury, or illness.

insurance policy A statement describing the terms of the contract between the insurance company and their client (the insured); it includes information on the costs of premiums and payouts and on the specific items covered by the insurance.

insurance premium An annual amount paid by the client or insured to purchase a specific amount of insurance.

long-term care The daily help needed by people who are elderly or by people with disabilities or serious illnesses, for example, nursing-home care.

Medicaid A health care program to assist low-income individuals and families in paying for medical expenses. It is paid for primarily by the federal government, with some input from the state.

medical benefit A service covered by the insurer; the insurer decides which benefits to offer, based on the average needs of patients.

medical necessity A treatment that a doctor considers essential; it may or may not be covered by insurance.

out-of-pocket expenses Medical expenses that are not covered by a patient's insurance and must be paid directly by the patient.

preexisting condition A medical condition that began before the person's insurance went into effect; until 2014, when the ACA went into effect, some companies refused to cover medical expenses from preexisting conditions.

preventive care Medical care designed to keep a person healthy; includes routine physical exams, regular screenings for certain diseases, and vaccinations.

provider network A group of health care providers that contract with a health insurance carrier, through an HMO or other group, to provide health care at a discount.

self-employed Working for oneself; working for a business that takes in income but has no employees.

short-term health insurance (temporary, or gap, insurance) Health insurance designed to last for a very short time (30–364 days) and used to provide insurance while the person is between policies.

single-payer health care A health care system in which the government pays for universal health care, usually through taxes.

subsidy Money that the government pays toward an expense; those with low incomes are offered a subsidy to help them afford health insurance premiums.

supplemental insurance Extra insurance bought to pay for out-of-pocket expenses or other expenses not covered by regular insurance; Medigap and cancer policies are examples.

universal health coverage (universal health care) A health care system that provides health care and financial protection for all members of a country's population.

FOR MORE INFORMATION

Canada Health Infoway
150 King Street West, Suite 1300
Toronto, ON M5H 1J9
Canada
(416) 979-4606 or (888) 733-6462
Website: https://www.infoway-inforoute.ca/en
Facebook: @CanadaHealthInfoway
Twitter: @Infoway
Canada Health Infoway is charged with accelerating adoption of digital health solutions, such as electronic health records, in Canada. It is independent, nonprofit, and federally funded.

Canadian Institute for Health Information (CIHI)
495 Richmond Road, Suite 600
Ottawa, ON K2A 4H6
Canada
(613) 241-7860
Website: https://www.cihi.ca/en
Facebook: @CIHI.ICIS
Twitter: @CIHI_ICIS
   CIHI is an independent, nonprofit organization that provides information on Canadian health systems and on the health of the Canadian people.

Centers for Medicare & Medicaid Services (CMS)
US Department of Health and Human Services
7500 Security Boulevard
Baltimore, MD 21244
(800) 706-7893
Website: https://www.cms.gov
Twitter: @CMSGov
YouTube: @CMSHHSgov
This government agency runs Medicare, Medicaid, and the Children's Health Insurance Program (CHIP). These sources have information on the services and on health issues.

Kaiser Family Foundation
185 Berry Street, Suite 2000
San Francisco, CA 94107
(650) 854-9400
Website: https://www.kff.org
Facebook: @KaiserFamilyFoundation
Twitter: @KaiserFamFound
This nonprofit organization focuses on health care issues in the United States and in global health policy. It provides facts, analysis, and polling on health care issues.

National Association of Health Underwriters (NAHU)
1212 New York Avenue NW, Suite 1100
Washington, DC 20005
(202) 552-5060

Facebook: @NationalAssociationofHealthUnderwriters
Twitter: @nahudotorg
NAHU is the major trade organization representing health insurance agents and brokers. It offers members educational opportunities, conferences, networking, publications, and more.

Social Security Administration
Office of Public Inquiries
1100 West High Rise
6401 Security Boulevard
Baltimore, MD 21235
(800) 772-1213
Website: https://www.ssa.gov
Facebook and Twitter: @SocialSecurity
This government agency provides financial protection to the retired, disabled, and survivors in the United States.

FOR FURTHER READING

Burnette, Josh, and Pete Hardesty. *Adulting 101: #Wisdom4Life*. Savage, MN: BroadStreet Publishing, 2018.

Hamilton, Robert M. *Should the Government Pay for Health Care?* New York, NY: KidHaven Publishing, 2020.

Harris, Duchess, and Rebecca Morris. *The Health-Care Divide*. Minneapolis, MN: Essential Library, 2019.

Heitkamp, Kristina Lyn, ed. *Universal Health Care*. New York, NY: Greenhaven Publishing, 2019.

McCoy, Erin L., and Corinne J. Naden. *Health Care: Universal Right or Personal Responsibility?*. Reprint ed. New York, NY: Cavendish Square, 2019.

Merino, Noël, ed. *Health Care*. Farmington Hills, MI: Greenhaven Publishing, 2015.

Pozen, Alexis, and Jim P. Stimpson. *Navigating Health Insurance*. Burlington, MA: Jones & Bartlett Learning, 2018.

Stevenson, Tyler. *Health Care. Limits, Laws, and Lives at Stake*. New York, NY: Lucent Press, 2019.

Stokes, Kathy E. *Insurance Operations*. Tinley Park, IL: Goodheart-Willcox, 2013.

Thompson, Tamara, ed. *The Affordable Care Act*. Farmington Hills, MI: Greenhaven Press, 2015.

BIBLIOGRAPHY

Baicker, Katherine. "Untitled." NEJM Catalyst. February 25, 2016. https://catalyst.nejm.org/videos/people-want-health-outcomes-not-health-care.

Business Benefits Group. "Everything You Need to Know About Group Health Insurance." Retrieved August 10, 2019. https://www.bbgbroker.com/group-health-insurance-explained.

Connolly, Dana. "The Future of US Healthcare: Haves vs. Have-Nots." The Hill, February 18, 2017. https://thehill.com/blogs/pundits-blog/healthcare/318563-us-is-headed-for-two-tiered-socialized-medicine-system.

Dorsey, Jenifer. "(Best) Health Insurance for Young Adults." Health eDeals, September 5, 2018. https://www.healthedeals.com/blog/save/young-adult-health-insurance.

Familydoctor.org. "Health Insurance: Understanding What It Covers." American Academy of Family Physicians. Retrieved April 11, 2019. https://familydoctor.org/health-insurance-understanding-covers.

Frayer, Lauren. "U.K. Hospitals Are Overburdened, but the British Love Their Universal Health Care." NPR, March 7, 2018. https://www.npr.org/sections/parallels/2018/03/07/591128836/u-k-hospitals-are-overburdened-but-the-british-love-their-universal-health-care.

HCC Medical Insurance Services Group. "Importance of Young Adult Health Insurance." Retrieved April 11, 2019. https://www.hccmis.com/short-term-insurance/importance-of-young-adult-health-insurance.

HealthCare.gov. "The 'Metal' Categories: Bronze, Silver, Gold, & Platinum." Retrieved February 26, 2019. https://www.healthcare.gov/choose-a-plan/plans-categories.

HealthCare.gov. "Out-of-Pocket Costs." Retrieved February 22, 2019. https://www.healthcare.gov/glossary/out-of-pocket-costs.

HHS.gov. "What Is the Difference Between Medicare and Medicaid?" October 2, 2015. https://www.hhs.gov/answers/medicare-and-medicaid/what-is-the-difference-between-medicare-medicaid/index.html.

Hiltzik, Michael. "The First Projections for Trumpcare 2019 Are In: Expect Rate Increases of Up to 30%." *Los Angeles Times*, January 26, 2018. https://www.latimes.com/business/hiltzik/la-fi-hiltzik-trumpcare-2019-story.html.

Kaiser Family Foundation. "Key Facts About the Uninsured Population." December 7, 2018. https://www.kff.org/uninsured/fact-sheet/key-facts-about-the-uninsured-population.

Kamal, Rabah, and Cynthia Cox. "How Do Healthcare Prices and Use in the U.S. Compare to Other Countries?" Peterson-Kaiser Health System Tracker, May 8, 2018. https://www.healthsystemtracker.org/chart-collection/how-do-healthcare-prices-and-use-in-the-u-s-compare-to-other-countries/#item-start.

Kleinbard, Edward D. "Do We Want Healthcare or Health Insurance?" The Hill, May 26, 2017. https://thehill.com/blogs/pundits-blog/healthcare/335151-do-we-want-healthcare-or-health-insurance.

Masterson, Les. "Different Types of Health Insurance Plans: Learn to Compare." Insurance.com, December 4, 2018. https://www.insurance.com/health-insurance/types-of-health-insurance.aspx.

McGuire, Colleen. "Meet the Metal Levels: Your Obamacare Cost Depends on Your Plan's Metal Name." HealthCare.com, September 18, 2017. https://www.healthcare.com/info/obamacare/obamacare-cost-insurance-plan-metal-level.

Merelli, Annalisa. "A History of Why the US is the Only Rich Country Without Universal Health Care." Quartz, July 18, 2017. https://qz.com/1022831/why-doesnt-the-united-states-have-universal-health-care.

ObamaCareFacts. "Facts on the Affordable Care Act." Obamacare Facts.com, February 28, 2019. https://obamacarefacts.com/obamacare-facts.

ObamaCareFacts. "Supplemental Health Insurance." Obamacare Facts.com, November 15, 2018. https://obamacarefacts.com/health-insurance/supplemental-health-insurance.

Sen, Amartya. "Universal Health Care: The Affordable Dream." *Harvard Public Health Review*. Retrieved April 24, 2019. http://harvardpublichealthreview.org/universal-health-care-the-affordable-dream.

Torrey, Tricia. "What You Should Know About Universal Health Care Coverage." VeryWell Health, November 26, 2018. https://www.verywellhealth.com/what-is-universal-healthcare-coverage-2615254.

Wood, Holly. "Unless You've Lived Without Health Insurance, You Have No Idea How Scary It Is." Vox, June 22, 2017. https://www.vox.com/first-person/2017/3/14/14907348/health-insurance-uninsured-ahca-obamacare.

INDEX

A

accidental death policy, 47–48
Affordable Care Act (ACA), 5–6, 14, 17, 18, 23, 28, 29, 35, 38, 39, 41, 44, 45, 46
Aflac, 44
asthma, 11

B

bankruptcy, resulting from medical costs, 6, 9, 26
benefits, types of, 9
blood pressure screening, 13
breast cancer screening, 13
bronze plan, 34, 35, 37

C

catastrophic health plans, 29, 41
cervical cancer screening, 13
Chandra, Alison, 26
children, preventive care for, 13
Children's Health Insurance Program (CHIP), 22–24
chronic illnesses, 11, 14, 49
claim, types of, 8–9
coinsurance, 9, 10, 37
Consolidated Omnibus Budget Reconciliation Act (COBRA) plan, 21
consumer-driven health plans (CDHPs), 22
co-pay, 9, 10, 23, 37, 45
critical illness insurance, 47

D

deductible, 9, 10, 17, 22, 26, 27, 37, 38, 45, 47, 48, 54
dental plans, 46
depression, 11, 13, 52
diabetes, 11, 13
dialysis, 26
domestic violence counseling, 13

E

epilepsy, 11
essential health benefits (EHBs), 14, 39, 53
exclusive provider organization (EPO), 20

F

Federal Poverty Level (FPL), 24
flu shot, 12

G

gold plan, 34, 35, 37
group health plans, 18–21, 22, 30, 44, 54

H

Health Cost Sharing, 42

INDEX

health exchange/marketplace, 28–29, 34, 39, 44, 54, 57
health insurance
　choosing a plan, 31, 33–35, 37–39, 41–43
　explanation of how it works, 7, 8
　reasons to have it, 11–14
　types of, 18–24, 26–30
　what is covered under, 14, 16
health maintenance organization (HMO), 20
heterotaxy syndrome, 26
human papillomavirus (HPV) vaccine, 13
hybrid plan, 51

I

in-service provider, 20

L

long-term care insurance, 49–53

M

major medical plans, 29
Medicaid, 17, 18, 22–24, 26, 35, 54, 57, 63
medical benefits, 16
medical necessities, 16
Medical Savings Account, 27
Medicare, 18, 22, 24, 26–27, 44, 49, 54, 57, 63
metal levels, 34–35, 37
multiple sclerosis, 35

National Health Service, 59, 63, 64
newborns, preventive care for, 13

O

open enrollment periods, 34
out-of-network providers, 20
out-of-pocket maximum, 10

P

penalties, for being uninsured under ACA, 14
platinum plan, 34, 35, 37
point of service (POS) plan, 20
preexisting medical conditions, 19, 41
preferred provider organizations (PPO), 20
premium, 8, 9, 13, 17, 22, 26, 27, 31, 33, 37, 38, 50
prenatal care, 24, 26
prescription medication coverage, 16, 27, 34, 41, 49
preventive care, 11–12, 13, 14, 17, 54, 60
private insurance, 18, 28–30
Professional Employer Organization, 42
provider networks, 19–20

qualified health plans, 29

S

self-employment, 41–42
silver plan, 34, 35, 37, 38
single-payer health care, 57, 59
Social Security, 26, 61
Social Security Disability Service, 27
student health plan, 38–39
subsidy, 9, 13, 17, 29, 34, 35, 38
Supplemental Security Income, 27
supplementary insurance plans, 18,
   34, 44–53, 54, 64

T

tax-exempt savings account, 22
teenagers, preventive care for, 13
temporary/short-term insurance
   plans, 18, 34, 39, 51–52

U

universal health care, 54, 57, 59–64
US health care, compared to other
   countries, 55–57, 59–65

V

vaccinations, 11, 12, 13, 17
vision plans, 46

W

women, preventive care for, 13
Wood, Holly, 4–5

ABOUT THE AUTHOR

Carol Hand has a PhD in zoology from the University of Georgia. Hand has taught college biology, written biology assessments for national assessment companies, and written middle and high school science curricula for a national company. She has authored many science books for young adults, including the biology titles *Introduction to Genetics*; *Epidemiology: The Fight against Ebola & Other Diseases*; and *Vaccines*.

PHOTO CREDITS

Cover LightField Studios/Shutterstock.com; pp. 5, 52 Monkey Business Images/Shutterstock.com; pp. 7, 18, 31, 44, 55 ESB Professional/Shutterstock.com; p. 8 Kaspars Grinvalds/Shutterstock.com; p. 10 PixelShot/Shutterstock.com; p. 12 MarkHatFeld/iStock/Getty Images; p. 15 Tyler Olson/Shutterstock.com; p. 19 Katherine Welles/Shutterstock.com; p. 21 John T Takai/Shutterstock.com; p. 23 Chicago Tribune/Tribune News Service/Getty Images; pp. 24–25 The Washington Post/Getty Images; pp. 28, 32–33 Joe Raedle/Getty Images; pp. 36–37 Odua Images/Shutterstock.com; p. 40 LifetimeStock/Shutterstock.com; p. 42 Flamingo Images/Shutterstock.com; p. 46 Corepics VOF/Shutterstock.com; p. 47 pikselstock/Shutterstock.com; p. 48 Michelle Del Guercio/Science Source; p. 51 Alexander Raths/Shutterstock.com; pp. 56, 60 Peterson-Kaiser Health System Tracker; p. 58 Anadolu Agency/Getty Images; p. 63 Andrew Aitchison/Corbis News/Getty Images.

Design and Layout: Jennifer Moy; Editors: Kathy Kuhtz Campbell and Wendy Wong; Photo Researcher: Sherri Jackson